*The*Power *of a* Vacation

Daily Travel Inspiration

365 Quotes, Verses, and Facts that Remind Us of
the Importance of Taking a Vacation

Compiled and Arranged by
AMY HINOTE

VRM Intel Magazine, LLC

ORDERING INFORMATION:
Quantity sales. Special discounts are available on quantity purchases by corporations, associations, and others. For details, contact
info@vrmintel.com

The Power of a Vacation, Amy Hinote. 1st ed., 2017
ISBN-13: 978-0-692-95057-9

"*The world is full of wonderful things you haven't seen yet. Don't ever give up on the chance of seeing them.*"

—J.K. Rowling

Dedicated to the men and women who work tirelessly in the vacation rental industry to facilitate millions of vacations in private homes. Your inspiring work allows travelers to create memories with their loved ones and to rejuvenate their minds, bodies, and souls. The world is a better place as a result of the vacation experiences you provide.

And to my many mentors, including J. Gary Ellis, who has done more to promote travel than anyone I know. His guidance shaped many careers and taught us all about the significance of leisure travel and the power of taking a vacation.

"Because I knew you, I have been changed for good."
—Stephen Schwartz

Contents

Introduction 9

January 13

February 25

March 37

April 49

May 61

June 73

July 85

August 97

September 109

October 121

November 133

December 145

About the Author 157

Introduction

In each of us lies an inner wanderer, a part of our souls, who yearns to go places we have never been, see things we have not yet seen, experience new pleasures and sensations, and discover horizons that forever change our perspective.

As human beings, we also have a need to escape our everyday lives. We crave leisurely mornings minus alarms. A fresh powdering of snow. Afternoons spent listening to the waves, our feet snuggled in sand, and moonlit nights under starry skies.

Travel allows us these luxuries; it grants us opportunities to live like someone else and to be someone else. Our travel experiences soon become a part of us. The person we discover within ourselves on the journey returns home and creates in us a new and more complex version of self.

Many do not realize how important these experiences are to our mental and physical health and to the well-being of our families, friends, and coworkers. We remain largely unaware of the importance of vacations that transform us, spark our creativity, and reignite our passion for living.

The verdict is in: leisure travel changes us—for the better.

As a fellow traveler, like you, I have experienced firsthand the way in which a journey can change a life. In the midst of the first of two yearlong road trips, I became aware that authors and poets across the centuries have articulated the significance of following our hearts and venturing beyond familiar paths. I realized that our need to wander and explore is timeless. Not only have hundreds of notable writers, poets, and philosophers long documented the wanderlust and soul growth that vacations provide, they have allowed us a glimpse into the physical and mental healing travel offers.

My parents recognized this early in life and understood the power of the vacation. Twice a year, our family spent incredible weeks in beach and mountain vacation rentals. On random weekends, my father took us on long drives along country back roads. We were not looking for the destination but for what we could learn from the journey itself.

My best and most vivid memories are spun from family vacations. The one-on-one time with my parents and brothers, the sights we enjoyed, and the bonds formed through our trips are a foundational part of who I am. The various, bizarre challenges we met and conquered along the way gave us colorful stories that we have passed down to the next generation of family travelers.

Our vacations take many forms. We rediscover our inner child in the excitement of theme parks. We are drawn to the sounds, smells, and stimulation of the city. We travel back in time to historic sites and embark on breathtaking adventures through canyons, white water, and mountain trails. We cross seas and zipline over forest treetops, and we vegetate on sandy beaches or read guilty fiction in flannel before a fire in a remote cabin.

This publication was originally designed to serve as a thank-you note and a book of encouragement to those whose careers are founded in the travel industry. The goal was to demonstrate to those who live and breathe vacations, through a compilation of quotes, facts, song, and verse, the significance of their daily work. These excerpts will remind them of how much the vacations they offer mean to those who enjoy them.

Through the editing process, however, I realized this book is not only valuable to travel providers but also serves to inspire people to travel and convey its importance to all of us.

Whether joining family and friends to get away from it all or venturing on solo journeys of self-discovery, vacationing alters our vision and adds new ingredients to the potpourri of who we are as individuals.

The authors, travelers, poets, songwriters, doctors, academics, and philosophers quoted in this book articulate in brilliant fashion the healing power of the vacation and the significance travel brings to our lives.

These pages contain daily discoveries and truths, sprinkled with bits of humor, of the importance of expanding our perspectives through travel. My hope is that the quotes in this book inspire you daily to move, wander, risk, and embark on more adventures.

No matter how small, each and every journey changes our trajectory, adds layers to our experiences on this planet, and gives us added perspective on the lives of others.

Through travel, we are able to see the world with fresh eyes and to comprehend that no matter the number of miles we roam, the mountains we climb, or the oceans we cross, our similarities far outshine our differences.

January

January 1

"It is in all of us to defy expectations, to go into the world and to be brave, and to want, to need, to hunger for adventures. To embrace the chance and risk so that we may breathe and know what it is to be free."

Mae Chevrette

January 2

"To move, to breathe, to fly, to float,
To gain all while you give,
To roam the roads of lands remote,
To travel is to live."

Hans Christian Andersen, *The Fairy Tale of My Life*

January 3

"Travel is fatal to prejudice, bigotry, and narrow-mindedness, and many of our people need it sorely on these accounts. Broad, wholesome, charitable views of men and things cannot be acquired by vegetating in one little corner of the earth all one's lifetime."

Mark Twain, *The Innocents Abroad*

January 4

"In matters of healing the body or the mind, vacation is a true genius!"

Mehmet Murat Ildan

January 5

"Climb every mountain,
Search high and low.
Follow every byway,
Every path you know."

Oscar Hammerstein II, *Sound of Music*

January 6

"Vacations are your best chance in the year to get in some real living, to get out of the job-as-life box, off automatic pilot, and rediscover your passions, enthusiasms, friends, family, and the vitality of partaking in the world outside career brainlock. Social scientists have found that leisure experiences increase positive mood, act as a buffer against life's setbacks, and open the door to the best times of our lives."

John De Graff, *Take Back Your Time*

January 7

A majority (52 percent) of workers who say they set aside time each year to plan out their vacation days take all their time off, compared to just 40 percent of non-planners. They also tend to take longer vacations.

The State of the American Vacation 2017

January 8

"Once the travel bug bites there is no known antidote, and I know that I shall be happily infected until the end of my life."

Michael Palin

January 9

"Adventure rewrites the routine of our lives and wakes us sharply from the comforts of the familiar. It allows us to see how vast the expanse of our experience. Our ability to grow is no longer linear but becomes unrestricted to any direction we wish to run."

Josh Gates, *Destination Truth: Memoirs of a Monster Hunter*

January 10

"Henceforth I ask not good-fortune,
    I myself am good-fortune,
Henceforth I whimper no more,
    postpone no more, need
    nothing,
Done with indoor complaints,
    libraries, querulous criticisms,
Strong and content I travel the open
    road."

Walt Whitman, *Songs of the Open Road*

January 11

"The impulse to travel is one of the hopeful symptoms of life."

Agnes Repplier

January 12

"Vacations brighten a man. They tend to make his work more attractive to him and to make him more attractive to his work."

Harry Van Demark

January 13

"Certainly, travel is more than the seeing of sights; it is a change that goes on, deep and permanent, in the ideas of living."

Mary Ritter Beard

January 14

"American workers hold fast to the belief that the path to career success requires sacrificing vacation and embracing work martyrdom. But the data is unmistakably clear: planning for and taking time off benefits individual well-being and professional success, business performance, and the broader economy."

The State of American Vacation 2017

January 15

"Why do you go away? So that you can come back. So that you can see the place you came from with new eyes and extra colors. And the people there see you differently, too. Coming back to where you started is not the same as never leaving."

Terry Pratchett, *A Hat Full of Sky*

January 16

"Travelling unveils new dimensions of this world not known to the naked eye."

Wayne Chirisa

January 17

"If I'm an advocate for anything, it's to move. As far as you can, as much as you can. Across the ocean, or simply across the river. The extent to which you can walk in someone else's shoes or at least eat their food, it's a plus for everybody.

"Open your mind, get up off the couch, move."

Anthony Bourdain

January 18

"Vacations are seen as an antidote to work. They are medicine, a remedy for counteracting the effects of labor.... Vacations allow us to be away from the job, to change the patterns of our day, to alter our routine, to reconfigure our actions and habits, to rediscover ourselves."

Al Gini, *The Importance of Being Lazy*

January 19

"One's destination is never a place, but a new way of seeing things."

Henry Miller

January 20

"But that's the glory of foreign travel, as far as I am concerned. I don't want to know what people are talking about. I can't think of anything that excites a greater sense of childlike wonder than to be in a country where you are ignorant of almost everything. Suddenly you are five years old again. You can't read anything, you have only the most rudimentary sense of how things work, you can't even reliably cross a street without endangering your life. Your whole existence becomes a series of interesting guesses."

Bill Bryson, *Neither Here Nor There*

January 21

"I'd like to dial it back 5 percent or 10 percent and try to have a vacation that's not just e-mail with a view."

Elon Musk

January 22

"Be bold and fly toward the unknown. Discover a road that was never known."

Debasish Mridha

January 23

"'You have not traveled enough,' she said. 'Or you'd know that every journey makes its own map across your heart.'"

Sharon Shinn, *Mystic and Rider*

January 24

"Travel improves the mind wonderfully, and does away with all one's prejudices."

Oscar Wilde, *The Happy Prince and Other Tales*

January 25

"Life is a journey to be experienced, not a problem to be solved."

Pooh, *Winnie the Pooh*

January 26

"A person does not grow from the ground like a vine or a tree, one is not part of a plot of land. Mankind has legs so it can wander."

Roman Payne, *The Wanderess*

January 27

"There is no happiness for him who does not travel, Rohita! Thus we have heard. Living in the society of men, the best man becomes a sinner...therefore, wander!...The fortune of him who is sitting, sits; it rises when he rises; it sleeps when he sleeps; it moves when he moves. Therefore, wander!"

Aitareya Brahmanan, *In the Rigveda*

January 28

"The pleasure we derive from journeys is perhaps dependent more on the mindset with which we travel than on the destination we travel to."

Alain de Botton, *The Art of Travel*

January 29

"Wherever you go becomes a part of you somehow."

Anita Desai

January 30

"Jobs fill your pockets, adventures fill your soul."

Jamie Lyn Beatty

January 31

"I took off for a weekend last month,
Just to try and recall the whole year.
All of the faces and all of the places,
Wonderin' where they all disappeared.
I didn't ponder the question too long;
I was hungry and went out for a bite.
Ran into a chum with a bottle of rum,
And we wound up drinkin' all night.

It's those changes in latitudes,
Changes in attitudes nothing remains quite the same.
With all of our running and all of our cunning,
If we couldn't laugh, we would all go insane."

Jimmy Buffett, *Changes in Latitudes, Changes in Attitude*

February

February 1

"The world is such a big place; staying in one town your whole life, is like never leaving your house."

Chris Geiger, *The Cancer Survivors Club*

February 2

"Learning to let go is not giving up! It is simply passing the burden to a better fighter, so you can fight another day."

Shannon L. Alder

February 3

The landmark Framingham Heart Study—the largest and longest-running study of cardiovascular disease—revealed that men who didn't take a vacation for several years were 30 percent more likely to have heart attacks compared to men who did take time off. And women who took a vacation only once every six years or less were almost eight times more likely to develop coronary heart disease or have a heart attack compared to women who vacationed at least twice a year.

Project: Time Off

February 4

"Now more than ever do I realize that I will never be content with a sedentary life, that I will always be haunted by thoughts of a sun-drenched elsewhere."

Isabelle Eberhardt, *The Nomad: The Diaries of Isabelle Eberhardt*

February 5

"The real danger of the vacation lies in its capacity to compress all family conflicts into an exquisitely focused drama."

Lance Morrow

February 6

"The most difficult thing is the decision to act, the rest is merely tenacity. The fears are paper tigers. You can do anything you decide to do. You can act to change and control your life; and the procedure, the process is its own reward. Adventure is worthwhile in itself."

Amelia Earhart

February 7

"Adventure is worthwhile."

Aristotle

February 8

"Travel is costly yes, but it pays dividends too."

Aaron Lauritsen, *100 Days Drive: The Great North American Road Trip*

February 9

"A vacation spot out of season always has a very special magic."

Max von Sydow

February 10

"A vacation is what you take when you can no longer take what you've been taking."

Earl Wilson

February 11

"…for every mile the feet go, the heart goes nine."

E.E. Cummings, *100 Selected Poems*

February 12

"Travel far enough, you meet yourself."

David Mitchell, *Cloud Atlas*

February 13

"You can fall in love at first sight with a place as well as a person."

Alec Waugh

February 14

A study by the Arizona Department of Health and Human Services found that women who took vacations were more satisfied with their marriages.

Healthy Set Go

February 15

"Travel brings power and love back into your life."

Jalaluddin Rumi

February 16

"The breaks you take from work pay you back manifold when you return because you come back with a fresher mind and newer thinking. Some of your best ideas come when you're on vacation."

Gautam Singhania

February 17

"The Road goes ever on and on
Down from the door where it began.
Now far ahead the Road has gone,
And I must follow, if I can,
Pursuing it with eager feet,
Until it joins some larger way
Where many paths and errands meet.
And whither then? I cannot say."

J.R.R. Tolkien, *The Fellowship of the Ring*

February 18

"The idea and experience of travel can mean many things: it involves movement of some kind, sometimes through unknown places, at other times just between home and the world. Journeys can also be inward, marking rites of passage or a growth into a new dimension. We travel in search of profit, pleasure or curiosity, to labour and survive, to flee from tyranny or sorrow, and into real and imagined utopias."

Teju Behan, *Drawing from the City*

February 19

"Being the people we are, and feeling the way that we do, getting excited about going somewhere new can be terrifying. Of course it is, I get it! But if you don't travel, you'll regret it. Your soul will forever be empty."

S.R. Crawford, *From My Suffering: 25 Ways to Break the Chains of Anxiety, Depression & Stress*

February 20

"A wise man travels to discover himself."

James Russell Lowell

February 21

"Focus on your destination but enjoy every sacred moment of the journey."

Lailah Gifty Akita, *Pearls of Wisdom: Great Mind*

February 22

"Climb the mountain not to plant your flag, but to embrace the challenge, enjoy the air and behold the view. Climb it so you can see the world, not so the world can see you."

David McCullough Jr.

February 23

"A journey is a person in itself; no two are alike. And all plans, safeguards, policies and coercion are fruitless.

"We find after years of struggle that we do not take a trip; a trip takes us."

John Steinbeck

February 24

"The holiest of all holidays are those
Kept by ourselves in silence and apart;
The secret anniversaries of the heart,
When the full river of feeling overflows;
The happy days unclouded to their close;
The sudden joys that out of darkness start
As flames from ashes; swift desires that dart
Like swallows singing down each wind that blows!
White as the gleam of a receding sail,
White as a cloud that floats and fades in air,
White as the whitest lily on a stream,
These tender memories are; —a fairy tale
Of some enchanted land we know not where,
But lovely as a landscape in a dream."

Henry Wadsworth Longfellow, *Holidays*

February 25

"Traveling is not just seeing the new; it is also leaving
behind. Not just opening doors; also closing them behind
you, never to return. But the place you have left forever is
always there for you to see whenever you shut your eyes."

Jan Myrdal

February 26

"What gives value to travel is fear. It breaks down a kind of inner structure we all have."

Elizabeth Benedict

February 27

"Travel makes one modest. You see what a tiny place you occupy in the world."

Gustave Flaubert

February 28

If Americans took all of the vacation they were entitled to instead of leaving days on the table every year, it would result in an additional 580 million more days of travel per year—a $160 billion boost to the economy.

Mental Floss

March

March 1

"We must leave this terrifying place tomorrow and go searching for sunshine."

F. Scott Fitzgerald

March 2

"Take time to leave cities, at least once in a year, and go to some natural place, hills, sea, jungles, rivers, where you see nothing but nature...His creations. Where you only hear chirping of birds, clinkering of trees, murmuring of winds, splashes of water in the river, and uproar of waterfalls."

Girdhar Joshi, *Some Mistakes Have No Pardon*

March 3

"Travel is life-changing. That's the promise made by a thousand websites and magazines, by philosophers and writers down the ages. Mark Twain said it was fatal to prejudice, and Thomas Jefferson said it made you wise. Anais Nin observed that 'we travel, some of us forever, to seek other states, other lives, other souls.' It's all true. Self-transformation is what I sought and what I found."

Elisabeth Eaves, *Wanderlust*

March 4

"Travel can also be the spirit of adventure somewhat tamed, for those who desire to do something they are a bit afraid of."

Ella Maillart

March 5

"…to travel is worth any cost or sacrifice."

Elizabeth Gilbert, *Eat, Pray, Love*

March 6

"Traveling outgrows its motives. It soon proves sufficient in itself. You think you are making a trip, but soon it is making you—or unmaking you."

Nicolas Bouvier, *The Way of the World*

March 7

"Travel like Ghandi, with simple clothes, open eyes and an uncluttered mind."

Rick Steves

March 8

"We live in a wonderful world that is full of beauty, charm and adventure. There is no end to the adventures we can have if only we seek them with our eyes open."

Jawaharlal Nehru

March 9

"The more that you read, the more things you will know. The more that you learn, the more places you will go."

Dr. Seuss

March 10

"Traveling is almost like talking with men of other centuries."

René Descartes

March 11

"Some trips are more than distance traveled in miles."

Lucy Knisley, *An Age of License: A Travelogue*

March 12

"Explore the world with an open mind, a sturdy carry-on, and clothes that don't wrinkle!"

Madeleine K. Albright, *Notes From My Travels*

March 13

"I see trees of green, red roses too,
I see them bloom for me and you,
And I think to myself what a wonderful world."

Louis Armstrong, *What a Wonderful World*

March 14

"But don't go trying to use the same route twice. Indeed, don't try to get there at all. It'll happen when you're not looking for it."

C.S. Lewis, *The Lion, The Witch and the Wardrobe*

March 15

"He who returns from a journey is not the same as he who left."

Chinese Proverb

March 16

"A journey, after all, neither begins in the instant we set out, nor ends when we have reached our door step once again. It starts much earlier and is really never over, because the film of memory continues running on inside of us long after we have come to a physical standstill. Indeed, there exists something like a contagion of travel, and the disease is essentially incurable."

Ryszard Kapuściński, *Travels with Herodotus*

March 17

"May you have the hindsight to know where you've been, the foresight to know where you're going, and the insight to know when you're going too far."

Irish Blessing

March 18

"He and I suddenly saw the whole country like an oyster for us to open; and the pearl was there, the pearl was there."

Jack Kerouac, *On the Road*

March 19

"We'd all be lucky in life if we had the chance to experience an unexpected adventure, and then make our way back safely to a place of comfort. Sometimes the only way we can appreciate our home and the simple happiness it has to offer is to be away from it for a while."

Noble Smith, *The Wisdom of the Shire: A Short Guide to a Long and Happy Life*

March 20

"Somewhere over the rainbow skies are blue,
And the dreams that you dare to dream really do come true."

Yip Harburg, *Wizard of Oz*

March 21

"Total physical and mental inertia are highly agreeable, much more so than we allow ourselves to imagine. A beach not only permits such inertia but enforces it, thus neatly eliminating all problems of guilt. It is now the only place in our overly active world that does."

John Kenneth Galbraith

March 22

"Roam abroad in the world, and take thy fill of its enjoyments before the day shall come when thou must quit it for good."

Saadi Shirazi

March 23

"Every dreamer knows that it is entirely possible to be homesick for a place you've never been to, perhaps more homesick than for familiar ground."

Judith Thurman

March 24

"Blessed be the man who invented vacations! Deeply as I am interested in education, much as I am attached to the young men whom Providence places under my instruction, and much as I find of interest in the sciences which it falls to my lot to teach, yet the annual return of the Summer vacation is always expected with pleasure and hailed with welcome."

Lawrence Larrabee, *The Ladies' Repository*, 1851

March 25

"Better to see something once than to hear about it a thousand times."

Asian Proverb

March 26

"Nostalgia in reverse, the longing for yet another strange land, grew especially strong in spring."

Vladimir Nabokov, *Mary*

March 27

"I've made a lot of stops all over the world,
And in every part I own the heart
Of at least one lovely girl."

Ricky Nelson, *Travelin' Man*

March 28

"There's something out there I can't resist."

Heart, *These Dreams*

March 29

"Your comfort zone is a place where you keep yourself in a self-illusion and nothing can grow there, but your potentiality can grow only when you can think and grow out of that zone."

Rashedur Ryan Rahman

March 30

"We must go beyond textbooks, go out into the bypaths and untrodden depths of the wilderness and travel and explore and tell the world the glories of our journey."

John Hope Franklin

March 31

"Two roads diverged in a wood, and I—
I took the one less traveled by,
And that has made all the difference."

Robert Frost, *The Road Less Traveled*

April

April 1

"Sometimes I travel just to be overwhelmed—for it's good every now and then to be overwhelmed."

Carew Papritz, *The Legacy Letters*

April 2

"A dominant impulse on encountering beauty is to wish to hold on to it, to possess it and give it weight in one's life. There is an urge to say, 'I was here, I saw this and it mattered to me.'"

Alain de Botton, *The Art of Travel*

April 3

"Far too many people on the spectrum spend most of their days with people who carry around memories of, and are often too overwhelmed by incidents of, prior misinterpretation. This is no fun. In travel you can start over, and reinvent yourself. If somehow a relationship gets weird, you can leave and go to the next town, the next block, or whatever the case may be, and try again."

Michael John Carley, *Asperger's From the Inside Out*

April 4

"I guess the lesson is you can't go everywhere. You should still go everywhere you can."

Charles Finch

April 5

"How will I know who I can become if I don't give myself the chance to try new things, to push myself beyond my natural boundaries? Who might I be if I am away from the things that I currently use to define myself?"

Eileen Cook, *With Malice*

April 6

"When you give yourself to places, they give you yourself back; the more one comes to know them, the more one seeds them with the invisible crop of memories and associations that will be waiting for you when you come back, while new places offer up new thoughts, new possibilities. Exploring the world is one the best ways of exploring the mind, and walking travels both terrains."

Rebecca Solnit, *Wanderlust: A History of Walking*

April 7

"Vacations tend to create memories more than any other family activity, and the bad times are some of the best memories."

William Doherty, University of Minnesota, Vacations Are *"Good for You, Medically Speaking."* New York Times

April 8

Scientists from the Icahn School of Medicine, University of California and Harvard found that just six days away triggers genetic changes which dampens stress, boosts the immune system and lowers levels of proteins linked to dementia and depression. "It's intuitive that taking a vacation reduces biological processes related to stress, but it was still impressive to see the large changes in gene expression from being away from the busy pace of life, in a relaxing environment, in such a short period of time. Our results point to both a significant 'vacation effect' that benefited all groups, and a suppression of stress-related responses."

Dr. Elissa Epel, Professor of Psychiatry at University of California, San Francisco

April 9

"Perhaps travel cannot prevent bigotry, but by demonstrating that all peoples cry, laugh, eat, worry, and die, it can introduce the idea that if we try and understand each other, we may even become friends."

Maya Angelou, *Wouldn't Take Nothing for My Journey Now*

April 10

"Travel is the only thing you buy that makes you richer."

Unknown

April 11

"Live life with no excuses and travel with no regrets."

Montel Williams

April 12

"Travel, in the younger sort, is a part of education; in the elder, a part of the experience."

Francis Bacon

April 13

"We wander for distraction, but we travel for fulfillment."

Hilaire Belloc

April 14

"With every journey there is a new lesson learned, every place traveled, explored; makes us fall in love with the earth. Care less about our whereabouts; we keep the expedition going because we want to go far beyond the civilized, beyond the living, beyond the world of predictability, beyond u and I and into the wild. Feasting the eyes, rejuvenating the senses, every breath we take is a sigh of relief and we make peace.

"Choosing the roads less traveled, our wandering souls make our way towards the unknown destination not only to discover ourselves but to discover the wild, nature and the mother earth."

Pushpa Rana, *Just the Way I Feel*

April 15

"Sometimes the road less traveled is less traveled for a reason."

Jerry Seinfeld

April 16

"Live vicariously through yourself."

Dayna Lovely

April 17

"Through travel I first became aware of the outside world; it was through travel that I found my own introspective way into becoming a part of it."

Eudora Welty, *One Writer's Beginnings*

April 18

"I travel not to go anywhere, but to go. I travel for travel's sake. The great affair is to move."

Robert Louis Stevenson

April 19

"Once a year, go somewhere you have never been before."

Dalai Lama

April 20

"Most travel, and certainly the rewarding kind, involves depending on the kindness of strangers, putting yourself into the hands of people you don't know and trusting them with your life."

Paul Theroux, *Ghost Train to the Eastern Star*

April 21

"What is more melancholy and more profound than to see a thousand objects for the first and the last time? To travel is to be born and to die at every instant..."

Victor Hugo, *Les Misérables*

April 22

"Reflecting on our happiest memories of joyful time spent together as a family can be extremely powerful in bringing relief and respite when faced with the darker times that life can bring."

John McDonald, Director of the Family Holiday Association

April 23

"Nobody can discover the world for somebody else. Only when we discover it for ourselves does it become common ground and a common bond and we cease to be alone."

Wendell Berry, *A Place on Earth*

April 24

"Traveling can never be taken for granted, no matter how meticulous the preparations."

Eugene Linden, *The Ragged Edge of the World*

April 25

"...there ain't no journey what don't change you some."

David Mitchell, *Cloud Atlas*

April 26

"With age, comes wisdom. With travel, comes understanding."

Sandra Lake

April 27

"I must go down to the sea again, for the call of the running tide, is a wild call and a clear call that cannot be denied!"

John Masefield

April 28

"Our happiest moments as tourists always seem to come when we stumble upon one thing while in pursuit of something else."

Lawrence Block

April 29

"I went skydiving,
I went Rocky Mountain climbing,
I went 2.7 seconds on a bull named Fumanchu.
And I loved deeper,
And I spoke sweeter,
And I gave forgiveness I'd been denying.
And he said, 'Someday I hope you get the chance
To live like you were dying.'"

Tim McGraw, *Live Like You Were Dying*

April 30

"And my mother, whose radius of travel was short, tied the letters with ribbon and kept them in her desk. When you get the chance, she said to me, 'go.'"

Frances Mayes, *A Year in the World*

May

May 1

"The advantage of travel is that after a while you begin to realize that wherever you go, most people aren't really all that much different."

Joanne Harris, *Chocolat*

May 2

"I like to believe that the road is sharpening my mind and lengthening my life with surprise."

Gloria Steinem

May 3

"Here today, up and off to somewhere else tomorrow! Travel, change, interest, excitement! The whole world before you, and a horizon that's always changing!"

Kenneth Grahame, *The Wind in the Willows*

May 4

"Paris is always a good idea."

Audrey Hepburn

May 5

"To me, travel is more valuable than any stupid piece of bling money can buy."

Raquel Cepeda, *Bird of Paradise*

May 6

"Each day of our lives we make deposits in the memory banks of our children."

Charles R. Swindoll

May 7

"If you can dream it, you can do it. Always remember, that this whole thing was started by a mouse."

Walt Disney

May 8

"All journeys have secret destinations of which the traveler is unaware."

Martin Buber

May 9

"Offline is the new luxury."

Unknown

May 10

"No man is brave that has never walked a hundred miles. If you want to know the truth of who you are, walk until not a person knows your name. Travel is the great leveler, the great teacher, bitter as medicine, crueler than mirror-glass. A long stretch of road will teach you more about yourself than a hundred years of quiet."

Patrick Rothfuss

May 11

"Those who are waiting to go on a holiday are much happier with their life as a whole, experience less negative or unpleasant feelings, and thus enjoy an overall net positive effect or pleasant feelings. The holiday-taking group are also happier with their family, economic situation and health."

David Gilbert and Junaida Abdullah, University of Surrey

May 12

"I want to get away,
I want to fly away.
Let's go and see the stars,
The milky way or even mars,
Where it could just be ours."

Lenny Kravitz, *Fly Away*

May 13

"A vacation frequently means that the family goes away
for a rest, accompanied by a mother who sees that the
others get it."

Marcelene Cox

May 14

"Please be a traveler, not a tourist. Try new things, meet
new people, and look beyond what's right in front of you.
Those are the keys to understanding this amazing world
we live in."

Andrew Zimmerman

May 15

"Build traditions of family vacations and trips and outings. These memories will never be forgotten by your children."

Ezra Taft Benson

May 16

"Don't tell me how educated you are, tell me how much you have travelled."

Anonymous

May 17

"You can't control the past, but you can control where you go next."

Kirsten Hubbard, *Wanderlove*

May 18

"To travel is to possess the world."

Burton Holmes

May 19

"The American dream, what we were taught was, grow up, own a car, own a house. I think that dream's completely changing. We were taught to keep up with the Joneses. Now we're sharing with the Joneses."

Brian Chesky

May 20

"Travel does this: it creates space that allows thoughts and memories to intrude and assert themselves with impunity. Smells and sights, the quality of light, the honk of a horn—can all act as touchstones when least expected."

Andrew McCarthy, *The Longest Way Home*

May 21

"If you're twenty-two, physically fit, hungry to learn and be better, I urge you to travel—as far and as widely as possible. Sleep on floors if you have to. Find out how other people live and eat and cook. Learn from them—wherever you go."

Anthony Bourdain, *Medium Raw*

May 22

The Framingham Heart Study, which started in 1948, researchers looked at questionnaires women in the study had filled out over 20 years about how often they took vacations. Those women who took a vacation once every six years or less were almost eight times more likely to develop coronary heart disease or have a heart attack than those who took at least two vacations a year.

Elaine Eaker, Eaker Epidemiology Enterprises

May 23

"Traveling is not something you're good at. It's something you do, like breathing."

Gayle Foreman

May 24

"All travel has its advantages. If the passenger visits better countries, he may learn to improve his own, and if fortune carries him to worse, he may learn to enjoy it."

Samuel Johnson, *A Journey to the Western Islands of Scotland and The Journal of a Tour to the Hebrides*

May 25

"To finish the moment, to find the journey's end in every step of the road, to live the greatest number of good hours, is wisdom."

Ralph Waldo Emerson

May 26

"Extend your vacation whenever possible."

A.D. Posey

May 27

"As you grow older, you learn a few things. One of them is to actually take the time you've allotted for vacation."

John Battelle

May 28

"I am not the same having seen the moon shine on the other side of the world."

Mary Anne Radmacher

May 29

"A ship in harbor is safe, but that is not what ships are built for."

John A. Shedd

May 30

"Travel...the best way to be lost...and found...all at the same time."

Brenna Smith

May 31

"Now, bring me that horizon."

Johnny Depp

June

June 1

"I am convinced that the greatest legacy we can leave our children are happy memories: those precious moments so much like pebbles on the beach that are plucked from the white sand and placed in tiny boxes that lay undisturbed on tall shelves until one day they spill out and time repeats itself, with joy and sweet sadness, in the child now an adult."

Og Mandino

June 2

"I learned a long time ago that trying to micromanage the perfect vacation is always a disaster. That leads to terrible times."

Anthony Bourdain

June 3

"I got my toes in the water, ass in the sand,
Not a worry in the world, a cold beer in my hand.
Life is good today."

Zach Brown, *Toes*

June 4

"When people went on vacation, they shed their home skins, thought they could be a new person."

Aimee Friedman, *Sea Change*

June 5

"At times, it almost felt like I was destined to take the trip, like all the people I met had somehow been waiting for me."

Nicholas Sparks, *The Choice*

June 6

"Removing yourself from the familiar and opting for the unfamiliar opens up the unknown. And within the unknown there are questions we have never asked ourselves; experiences we have never imagined; lessons we have never had a chance to learn. What we ultimately need when we are stuck within a bubble, is change. Another perspective of seeing and knowing what is possible. Traveling will open that up for you. The world will play its role; all you need to do is pack your bags and allow it to happen."

Jellis Vaes

June 7

"There is a kind of magicness about going far away and then coming back all changed."

Kate Douglas Wiggin, *New Chronicles of Rebecca*

June 8

"Don't let your luggage define your travels, each life unravels differently."

Shane L. Koyczan

June 9

"Leave my cares behind,
Take my own sweet time,
Ocean's on my mind."

Jimmy Buffett, *Take Another Road*

June 10

"I haven't been everywhere, but it's on my list."

Unknown

June 11

"One of the gladdest moments of human life, me thinks, is the departure upon a distant journey into unknown lands. Shaking off with one mighty effort the fetters of habit, the leaden weight of routine, the cloak of many cares and the slavery of home, man feels once more happy."

Sir Richard Burton

June 12

"No one likes a straight road but the man who pays for it, or who, when he travels, is brute enough to wish to get to his journey's end."

J. Sheridan Le Fanu, *The Haunted Baronet And Others: Ghost Stories 1861-70*

June 13

"Certainly, travel is more than the seeing of sights; it is a change that goes on, deep and permanent, in the ideas of living."

Miriam Beard

June 14

"I have never believed that vacations are luxuries. They are our necessities—just like shelter, clothes, and food, they make us feel like humans and not like animals that care only for survival."

Alexander Babinets

June 15

"The older I got the more I appreciated the role of travel as a stimulus to memories, and the way in which journeys even to new places were somehow always awakening memories of places seen in an ever-receding past."

Michael Jacobs, *The Robber of Memories*

June 16

"It's in those quiet little towns, at the edge of the world, that you will find the salt of the earth people who make you feel right at home."

Aaron Lauritsen, *100 Days Drive: The Great North American Road Trip*

June 17

"I have an insane calling to be where I'm not."

Unknown

June 18

"It is easier to bear the worries of wandering than to find peace in your hometown, where only the sage can live in a happy house surrounded by trite troubles and daily distractions."

Hermann Hesse

June 19

"Happiness is making plans for the next vacation in the middle of an existing one."

Unknown

June 20

"Time you enjoy wasting is not wasted time."

Marthe Troly-Curtin

June 21

"A vacation is like love—anticipated with pleasure, experienced with discomfort, and remembered with nostalgia."

Unknown

June 22

"We travel not to escape life, but for life not to escape us."

Anonymous

June 23

"I will not follow where the path may lead, but I will go where there is no path, and I will leave a trail."

Muriel Strode

June 24

"We don't receive wisdom; we must discover it for ourselves after a journey that no one can take for us or spare us."

Marcel Proust

June 25

"One must travel, to learn. Every day, now, old Scriptural phrases that never possessed any significance for me before, take to themselves a meaning."

Mark Twain, *The Innocents Abroad*

June 26

"Then they said, 'Ask God whether or not our journey will be successful.' 'Go in peace,' the priest replied. 'For the Lord is watching over your journey.'"

Judges 18:5-6

June 27

"Bizarre travel plans are dancing lessons from God."

Kurt Vonnegut

June 28

"Travel with the wit of an adult, and the wonder of a child."

Anonymous

June 29

"Keep things on your trip in perspective, and you'll be amazed at the perspective you gain on things back home while you're away...One's little world is put into perspective by the bigger world out there."

Gail Rubin Bereny

June 30

"Travel is intensified living...and one of the last great sources of legal adventure."

Rick Steves

July

July 1

"The happiest memory of 49 percent of those surveyed was on vacation with family. A third of the respondents said they can still vividly remember their childhood family vacations, and a quarter of them copped to using such memories to get them through tough times."

Family Holiday Association, 2017

July 2

"All great literature is one of two stories; a man goes on a journey or a stranger comes to town."

Leo Tolstoy

July 3

"Journeys, like artists, are born and not made. A thousand differing circumstances contribute to them, few of them willed or determined by the will—whatever we may think. They flower spontaneously out of the demands of our natures—and the best of them lead us not only outwards in space, but inwards as well. Travel can be one of the most rewarding forms of introspection...."

Lawrence Durrell, *Bitter Lemons of Cyprus*

July 4

"I saw in their eyes something I was to see over and over in every part of the nation—a burning desire to go, to move, to get under way, anyplace, away from any Here. They spoke quietly of how they wanted to go someday, to move about, free and unanchored, not toward something but away from something. I saw this look and heard this yearning everywhere in every state I visited. Nearly every American hungers to move."

John Steinbeck, *Travels with Charley: In Search of America*

July 5

"Travel is a joy, full of surprises. Perhaps some of the most enjoyable times are those where one comes close to disaster: the risks add spice, and make for great stories when you are safely back home again."

Jane Wilson-Howarth, *How to Shit Around the World*

July 6

"I began to need my trips like other people need religion."

Kristin Newman

July 7

"There is nothing like returning to a place that remains unchanged to find the ways in which you yourself have altered."

Nelson Mandela

July 8

"We take to the breeze, we go as we please."

E.B. White, *Charlotte's Web*

July 9

"A vacation is having nothing to do and all day to do it in."

Robert Orben

July 10

"It is not the destination where you end up but the mishaps and memories you create along the way!"

Penelope Riley, *Travel Absurdities*

July 11

"We're ten hours from the ****ing fun park and you want to bail out. Well I'll tell you something. This is no longer a vacation. It's a quest. It's a quest for fun. You're gonna have fun, and I'm gonna have fun... We're all gonna have so much ****ing fun we're gonna need plastic surgery to remove our ****ing smiles! You'll be whistling 'Zip-A-Dee Doo-Dah' out of your ***holes!"

Clark Griswold, *National Lampoon's Vacation*

July 12

"You can shake the sand from your shoes, but not from your soul."

Unknown

July 13

"And if travel is like love, it is, in the end, mostly because it's a heightened state of awareness, in which we are mindful, receptive, undimmed by familiarity and ready to be transformed. That is why the best trips, like the best love affairs, never really end."

Pico Iyer

July 14

"Life should not be a journey to the grave with the intention of arriving safely in a pretty and well preserved body, but rather to skid in broadside in a cloud of smoke, thoroughly used up, totally worn out, and loudly proclaiming, 'Wow! What a Ride!'"

Hunter S. Thompson, *The Proud Highway*

July 15

Stress can contribute to heart disease and high blood pressure. For both men and women, the *New York Times* reported, taking a vacation every two years compared to every six will lessen the risk of coronary heart disease or heart attacks.

Healthy Set Go

July 16

"Twenty years from now you will be more disappointed by the things you didn't do than by the ones you did do. So throw off the bowlines. Sail away from the safe harbor. Catch the trade winds in your sails. Explore. Dream. Discover."

Mark Twain

July 17

The negative ion-rich oxygen found in nature also has a relaxing effect on the body. To put things in perspective, the Los Angeles freeway has a negative ion count of below 100 per cubic centimeter, while the area around a large waterfall can boast a negative ion count of 100,000 per cubic centimeter (average fresh air has 2,000-4,000 negative ions per cubic centimeter). Negatively ionized air promotes alpha brain waves and increases brain wave amplitude, which creates an overall clear and calming effect.

Mental Floss

July 18

"We travel not just to see the beauty of new places but to see our own beauty in a new environment."

Debasish Mridha

July 19

"Expectation is the dirtiest word in a traveler's vocabulary."

John Early, *Tales of the Modern Nomad*

July 20

"Each person deserves a day away in which no problems are confronted, no solutions searched for."

Maya Angelou, *Wouldn't Take Nothing for My Journey*

July 21

"Adventure is allowing the unexpected to happen to you. Exploration is experiencing what you have not experienced before. How can there be any adventure, any exploration, if you let somebody else—above all, a travel bureau—arrange everything before-hand?"

Richard Aldington, *Death of a Hero*

July 22

"Travel does what good novelists also do to the life of everyday, placing it like a picture in a frame or a gem in its setting, so that the intrinsic qualities are made more clear. Travel does this with the very stuff that everyday life is made of, giving to it the sharp contour and meaning of art."

Freya Stark

July 23

"And then I saw what I was to see so many times on the journey—a look of longing. 'Lord! I wish I could go!'
'Don't you like it here?'
'Sure. It's all right, but I wish I could go.'
'You don't even know where I'm going.'
'I don't care. I'd like to go anywhere.'"

John Steinbeck, *Travels with Charley*

July 24

"Travel makes me feel like a bird,
Travel gives me a sense of freedom,
Travel makes me come alive!"

Archana Chaurasia Kapoor

July 25

"The longing to get away from it all never was so great as in our present time of tension and trouble. We want something to lift us out of the mess into which much of life seems to have fallen."

Glenn Stewart

July 26

"The real voyage of discovery consists not in seeking new landscapes, but in having new eyes."

Marcel Proust

July 27

"I was to look around me as though I had never been in this place before. And slowly, my travels began to bear fruit."

Alain de Botton, *The Art of Travel*

July 28

"There's more to see than can ever be seen, more to do than can ever be done."

Tim Rice, *"Circle of Life,"* *The Lion King*

July 29

"The journey not the arrival matters."

T.S. Eliot

July 30

"See the world. It's more fantastic than any dream made or paid for in factories. Ask for no guarantees, ask for no security."

Ray Bradbury, *Fahrenheit 451*

July 31

"When people ask me why I still have hope and energy after all these years, I always say: Because I travel."

Gloria Steinem, *My Life on the Road*

August

August 1

"Here's what I love about travel: strangers get a chance to amaze you. Sometimes a single day can bring a blooming surprise, a simple kindness that opens a chink in the brittle shell of your heart and makes you a different person when you go to sleep—more tender, less jaded—than you were when you woke up."

Tanya Shaffer

August 2

"Wandering re-establishes the original harmony which once existed between man and the universe."

Anatole France

August 3

"The very basic core of a man's living spirit is his passion for adventure. The joy of life comes from our encounters with new experiences, and hence there is no greater joy than to have an endlessly changing horizon, for each day to have a new and different sun."

Christopher McCandless

August 4

"When preparing to travel, lay out all your clothes and all your money. Then take half the clothes and twice the money."

Susan Heller

August 5

"Travel early and travel often. Live abroad if you can. Understand cultures other than your own. As your understanding of other cultures increases, your understanding of yourself and your own culture will increase exponentially."

Tom Freston

August 6

"Travel has a way of stretching the mind. The stretch comes not from travel's immediate rewards, the inevitable myriad new sights, smells and sounds, but with experiencing firsthand how others do differently what we believed to be the right and only way."

Ralph Crawshaw

August 7

"Do not follow where the path may lead. Go instead where there is no path and leave a trail."

Ralph Waldo Emerson

August 8

"I dislike feeling at home when I am abroad."

George Bernard Shaw

August 9

"Take vacations, go as many places as you can. You can always make money, you can't always make memories."

Unknown

August 10

"Memories made on vacation stay in our hearts forever."

Unknown

August 11

"I'm leavin' on a jet plane,
I don't know when I'll be back again,
Oh, babe, I hate to go."

Peter, Paul and Mary, *Leavin' on a Jet Plane*

August 12

"Vacation time is something we all accrue, but only the wisest of us recognize its importance."

Andrea Goeglein

August 13

"The destination is not the journey. The destination is the person you choose to enjoy the journey with."

Shannon L. Alder

August 14

"Life was meant for good friends and great adventures."

Unknown

August 15

"A traveler without observation is a bird without wings."

Saadi Shirazi

August 16

"Here was something I already knew to be true about myself: Just as there are some wives who will occasionally need a break from their husbands in order to visit a spa for the weekend with their girlfriends, I will always be the sort of wife who occasionally needs a break from her husband in order to visit Cambodia. Just for a few days!"

Elizabeth Gilbert, *Committed: A Skeptic Makes Peace with Marriage*

August 17

"What I've learned from my travels is that people are more alike than they are different. Yes, I may have a different home or lifestyle than a mom living in Shanghai, but deep down we are still mothers who hope for the best in our children. I always find so much in common with those I meet on my travels—and that provides a genuine connection that cultural differences can't erase."

Janna Graber

August 18

"Traveling is a brutality. It forces you to trust strangers and to lose sight of all that familiar comfort of home and friends.

You are constantly off balance. Nothing is yours except the essential things: air, sleep, dreams, sea, the sky—all things tending towards the eternal or what we imagine of it."

Cesare Pavese

August 19

The odds of depression and tension were higher among women who took vacations only once in two years or once in six years compared to women who took vacations twice or more per year. The odds of marital satisfaction decreased as the frequency of vacations decreased.

Conclusion: Women who take vacations frequently are less likely to become tense, depressed, or tired, and are more satisfied with their marriage. These personal psychological benefits that lead to increased quality of life may also lead to improved work performance.

Vatsal Chikani, Douglas Reding, Paul Gunderson, Catherine A McCarty, Arizona Department of Health Services

August 20

"Let the sea breeze blow your hair, let the sunset bring tranquility to your heart, let the distant places you travel allow you to explore yourself."

Somya Kedia

August 21

"May my soul forever stay wild and my spirit always be adventurous."

Zascha Friis

August 22

"A good traveler has no fixed plans and is not intent on arriving."

Lao Tzu

August 23

"You must go on adventures to find out where you belong."

Sue Fitzmaurice

August 24

"Just got back from a pleasure trip: I took my mother-in-law to the airport."

Henny Youngman

August 25

"Only it seems to me that once in your life before you die you ought to see a country where they don't talk in English and don't even want to."

Thornton Wilder, *Our Town*

August 26

"One does not travel, any more than one falls in love, to collect material. It is simply part of one's life..."

Evelyn Wa

August 27

"He who is outside his door has the hardest part of his journey behind him."

Dutch Proverb

August 28

"The purpose of life is to live it, to taste experience to the utmost, to reach out eagerly and without fear for newer and richer experience."

Eleanor Roosevelt

August 29

"The cure for almost anything is salt water—sweat, tears, or the sea."

Isak Denison, *Out of Africa*

August 30

"Travel is the best school; it has the best teachers because everything seen is a teacher; and this colourful school's diploma is wisdom!"

Mehmet Murat Ildan

August 31

"No matter what happens, travel gives you a story to tell."

Jewish Proverb

September

September 1

The clear majority of managers agree that vacation improves health and well-being (82 percent), boosts morale (82 percent), and alleviates burnout (81 percent). Managers also believe in the benefits to the company: 78 percent say that vacation improves employees' focus upon return; 70 percent agree it renews employees' commitment to their job; and 64 percent feel it makes employees more willing to put in long hours when they are needed.

The State of American Vacation 2017

September 2

"What he sought was always something lying ahead, and even if it was a matter of the past it was a past that changed gradually as he advanced on his journey, because the traveler's past changes according to the route he has followed: not the immediate past, that is, to which each day that goes by adds a day, but the more remote past. Arriving at each new city, the traveler finds again a past of his that he did not know he had: the foreignness of what you no longer are or no longer possess lies in wait for you in foreign, unpossessed places."

Italo Calvino, *Invisible Cities*

September 3

"Once you have traveled, the voyage never ends, but is played out over and over again in the quietest chambers. The mind can never break off from the journey."

Pat Conroy

September 4

Parents report that they plan family vacations in order to provide their children with experiences they will remember for years to come. Three in every four (76 percent) parents believe that family vacations are worth the time and money because they "give my child experiences that they will remember years down the road."

Project Time Off, *Family Vacations Create Lasting Memories*

September 5

"No man needs a vacation so much as the man who has just had one."

Elbert Hubbard

September 6

"My ideal travel companions are my family."

Pharrell Williams

September 7

"At a time when so many people are just checking things off a bucket list, other travelers are finding that they want more."

Nicholas Kontis, *Going Local: Experiences and Encounters on the Road*

September 8

"Travel brings wisdom only to the wise. It renders the ignorant more ignorant than ever."

Joe Abercrombie, *Last Argument of Kings*

September 9

"Never go on trips with anyone you do not love."

Ernest Hemingway

September 10

"I believe in the sand beneath my toes.
The beach gives a feeling,
An earthy feeling,
I believe in the faith that grows."

Third Eye Blind, *Semi-Charmed Life*

September 11

"Life is short and the older you get, the more you feel it.
Indeed, you begin to realize how short life is. Almost
everyone has at least one friend who left the planet too
soon. People lose their capacity to walk, run, think, and
experience life. I realize how important it is to use the
time I have to see as much of the world as I can."

Nicholas Kontis

September 12

"Some journeys take us far from home. Some adventures
lead us to our destiny."

C.S. Lewis, *The Lion, the Witch, and the Wardrobe*

September 13

"To vacation in a rental home is a binary experience. Mountain cabin, beach house, New York City condo or cottage in the Cotswolds, a common thread weaves throughout. Two sets of people love the place: the owners who invest in, maintain and equip the home, primarily for the use of others; and the travelers who anticipate the trip, make lifelong memories while there, and, for one or two brief weeks each year, believe it is theirs. In that belief lies the secret of the success the vacation rental industry enjoys."

Ren Alford Hinote

September 14

"In the moment of decision, may you hear the voice of the Creator saying, 'This is right road, travel on it.'"

Lailah Gifty Akita, *Pearls of Wisdom*

September 15

"I hoped that the trip would be the best of all journeys: a journey into ourselves."

Shirley MacLaine

September 16

"Time well spent results in more money to spend, more money to save, and more time to vacation."

Zig Ziglar

September 17

"Travel is rich with learning opportunities, and the ultimate souvenir is a broader perspective."

Rick Steves

September 18

"If you reject the food, ignore the customs, fear the religion and avoid the people, you might better stay home."

James Michener

September 19

"Traveling in the company of those we love is home in motion."

Leigh Hunt

September 20

"The best way to get to know the place you are traveling in is to walk around...and the best way to walk around is in comfortable shoes! Grab your travel buddy and your running shoes and go explore!"

Laura Murano

September 21

"You have brains in your head.
You have feet in your shoes.
You can steer yourself
any direction you choose.
You're on your way. And you know what you know.
And YOU are the guy who'll decide where to go."

Dr. Seuss, *Oh The Places You'll Go!*

September 22

"My spirit has pass'd in compassion and determination around the whole earth. I have look'd for equals and lovers and found them ready for me in all lands, I think some divine rapport has equalized me with them."

Walt Whitman, *Leaves of Grass*

September 23

"He who does not travel does not know the value of men."

Moorish Proverb

September 24

"Travel is as much a passion as ambition or love."

Letitia Elizabeth Landon, *Romance and Reality*

September 25

"We cannot discover new oceans unless we have the courage to lose sight of the shore."

Andre Gide

September 26

"Traveling-to-a-place energy and living-in-a-place energy are two fundamentally different energies."

Elizabeth Gilbert, *Eat, Pray, Love*

September 27

One study found that three days after vacation, subjects' physical complaints, quality of sleep, and mood had improved as compared to before vacation. These gains were still present five weeks later, especially in those who had more personal time and overall satisfaction during their vacation.

Healthy Set Go

September 28

"To get away from one's working environment is, in a sense, to get away from one's self; and this is often the chief advantage of travel and change."

Charles Horton Cooley, *Social Organization: A Study of the Larger Mind*

September 29

"Why travel? To be changed, and to be changed again and again."

Carew Papritz, *The Legacy Letters*

September 30

"All good people agree,
And all good people say,
All nice people, like Us, are We,
And everyone else is They:
But if you cross over the sea,
Instead of over the way,
You may end by (think of it!) looking on We
As only a sort of They!"

Rudyard Kipling, *We and They*

October

October 1

"It's time to change my life and see the world."

Jennifer Coletta

October 2

"He who has never left his hearth and has confined his researches to the narrow field of the history of his own country cannot be compared to the courageous traveller who has worn out his life in journeys of exploration to distant parts and each day has faced danger in order to persevere in excavating the mines of learning and in snatching precious fragments of the past from oblivion."

Al-Mas'udi, *From the Meadows of Gold*

October 3

"I may stay here in this town another day or I may go on to another town. No one knows where I am. I am taking this bath in life, as you see, and when I have had enough of it I shall go home feeling refreshed."

Sherwood Anderson, *Death in the Woods and Other Stories*

October 4

"On the road again,
Goin' places that I've never been,
Seein' things that I may never see again,
And I can't wait to get on the road again."

Willie Nelson, *On the Road Again*

October 5

"The freedom of the open road is seductive,
serendipitous and absolutely liberating."

Aaron Lauritsen, *100 Days Drive*

October 6

"Such were our minor preparations for the journey, but
above all we laid in an ample stock of good-humour, and
a genuine disposition to be pleased; determining to travel
in true contrabandista style; taking things as we found
them, rough or smooth, and mingling with all classes and
conditions in a kind of vagabond companionship. It is the
true way to travel in Spain."

Washington Irving, *Tales of the Alhambra*

October 7

"Stop worrying about the potholes in the road and enjoy the journey."

Babbs Hoffman

October 8

"Reminds me of my safari in Africa. Somebody forgot the corkscrew and for several days we had to live on nothing but food and water."

W.C. Fields

October 9

"The feeling of a place was the best reason to go."

Robert Kurson, *Pirate Hunters*

October 10

"Vacations are necessities, not luxuries."

Linda Bloom, *101 Things I Wish I Knew When I Got Married*

October 11

"If adventures will not befall a young lady in her own village, she must seek them abroad."

Jane Austen, *Northanger Abbey*

October 12

"Make voyages. Attempt them. There's nothing else."

Tennessee Williams, *Camino Real*

October 13

"It all takes time and lessons and places, but I'm learning to listen to my restless heart, telling me to 'go, go, go!'"

Charlotte Eriksson

October 14

"It's a dangerous business, Frodo, going out your door. You step onto the road, and if you don't keep your feet, there's no knowing where you might be swept off to."

J.R.R. Tolkien, *The Fellowship of the Ring*

October 15

Three days after vacation, physical complaints, the quality of sleep and mood had improved as compared to before vacation. Average life satisfaction did not change during vacation. Five weeks after vacation subjects still reported less physical complaints than before vacation.

G, Strauss-Blasche, C. Ekmekcioglu, W. Marktl, US National Library of Medicine National Institutes of Health, *Study: Does Vacation Enable Recuperation?*

October 16

"Travel is rebellion in its purest form.

- we follow our heart
- we free ourselves of labels
- we lose control willingly
- we trade a role for reality
- we love the unfamiliar
- we trust strangers
- we own only what we can carry
- we search for better questions, not answers
- we truly graduate
- we, sometimes, choose never to come back."

Anonymous

October 17

"It was during my enchanted days of travel that the idea came to me, which, through the years, has come into my thoughts again and again and always happily—the idea that geology is the music of the earth."

Hans Cloos, *Conversation with the Earth*

October 18

"If travel has momentum and wants to stay in motion, as I mentioned earlier, then adventure has the gravitational pull of a black hole. The more you do it, the more you find a way to keep doing it."

Josh Gates, *Destination Truth: Memoirs of a Monster Hunter*

October 19

"If our lives are dominated by a search for happiness, then perhaps few activities reveal as much about the dynamics of this quest—in all its ardour and paradoxes— than our travels."

Alain de Botton, *The Art of Travel*

October 20

"So if you care to find me,
Look to the Western sky!
As someone told me lately,
Everyone deserves the chance to fly."

Elphaba, *Wicked*

October 21

"I'm flying,
Look at me way up high.
Suddenly here am I,
I'm flying."

Peter Pan, *I'm Flying*

October 22

"Leave home, leave the country, leave the familiar. Only then can routine experience—buying bread, eating vegetables, even saying hello—become new all over again."

Anthony Doerr

October 23

"Now, on this road trip, my mind seemed to uncrinkle, to breathe, to present to itself a cure for a disease it had not, until now, known it had."

Elizabeth Berg

October 24

"I don't know what you could say about a day in which you have seen four beautiful sunsets."

John Glenn

October 25

"'What shall you do all your vacation?" asked Amy. 'I shall lie abed and do nothing', replied Meg."

Louisa May Alcott, *Little Women*

October 26

"The one who doesn't travel, does not live."

Petar II Petrović Njegoš

October 27

"So shut up, live, travel, adventure, bless and don't be sorry."

Jack Kerouac, *Desolation Angels*

October 28

"Delay and dirt are the realities of the most rewarding travel."

Paul Theroux, *Ghost Train to the Eastern Star*

October 29

"A travel adventure has no substitute. It is the ultimate experience, your one big opportunity for flair."

Rosalind Massow

October 30

"Sensitive people feel so deeply they often have to retreat from the world, in order to dig beneath the layers of pain to find their faith and courage."

Shannon L. Alder

October 31

"And that's the wonderful thing about family travel: it provides you with experiences that will remain locked forever in the scar tissue of your mind."

Dave Barry

November

November 1

"The geographical pilgrimage is the symbolic acting out an inner journey."

Thomas Merton

November 2

"The everyday kindness of the back roads more than makes up for the acts of greed in the headlines."

Charles Kuralt

November 3

"She wasn't where she had been. She wasn't where she was going, but she was on her way."

Jodi Hills

November 4

"The best part of traveling is finding yourself."

Ken Poirot

November 5

"A journey—whether it's to the corner grocery or through life—is supposed to have a beginning, middle, and end, right? Well, the road is not like that at all. It's the very illogic and the juxtaposed differences of the road—combined with our search for meaning—that make travel so addictive."

Gloria Steinem, *My Life on the Road*

November 6

"A study, published in the Journal of Psychosomatic Medicine, which analyzed the relationship between death rates and frequency of vacations. They examined the data from the MRFIT trial, which studied heart disease risk factors in over twelve thousand men. During the five years of the trial, they kept track of how many vacations each person took, and then followed them for nine years after the trial ended. Controlling for all other factors, they discovered that taking multiple vacations, up to five a year, resulted in a 32 percent lower chance of death from all causes, compared to the men who didn't take vacations. The verdict: skipping vacations could actually kill you."

Susan Biali, M.D., *Prescription for Life*

November 7

"...take in the scenery, experience love, and learn what is important in this world: people, places, memories—not things or perceptions."

Sarah Reijonen

November 8

"The great glory of travel, to me, is not just what I see that's new to me in countries visited, but that in almost every one of them I change from an outsider looking in to an insider looking out."

Clara E. Laughlin, *Traveling Through Life*

November 9

"Isn't it interesting that people feel best about themselves right before they go on vacation? They've cleared up all of their to-do piles, closed up transactions, renewed old promises with themselves. My most basic suggestion is that people should do that more than just once a year."

David Allen

November 10

"A whole new world,
A new fantastic point of view.
No one to tell us no,
Or where to go,
Or say we're only dreaming.
A whole new world,
A dazzling place I never knew,
But when I'm way up here,
It's crystal clear,
That now I'm in a whole new world with you."

Lea Salonga, Brad Kane, *A Whole New World*

November 11

"I know, in my soul, that a love for travel is a gift and not a hindrance. It feels like a burden when the bucket list is bigger than the bank account, but a thirst for more of the world is not something to apologize for. Denying its presence feels like denying something good in me, something God put there. Wanderlust has a reputation as the epitome of unrequited love, something the young and naive chase after because they don't yet realize it's as futile as a dog chasing its tail. Turns out, ever-burning wanderlust is a good thing."

Tsh Oxenreider, *At Home in the World*

November 12

"My best vacation is somewhere I could hide, somewhere warm and not a lot of people around."

Derek Jeter

November 13

"One of the great things about travel is that you find out how many good, kind people there are."

Edith Wharton

November 14

Employees who forfeit their vacation days do not perform as well as those who use all their time. While they may believe sacrificing vacation time will get them ahead, these employees are less likely than non-forfeiters to have been promoted within the last year (23 percent to 27 percent) and to have received a raise or bonus in the last three years (78 percent to 84 percent). This is on top of the $66.4 billion in benefits they lost by forfeiting time last year.

The State of American Vacation 2017

November 15

"A journey is like marriage. The certain way to be wrong is to think you control it."

John Steinbeck

November 16

"You lose sight of things... and when you travel, everything balances out."

Daranna Gidel

November 17

"Whoever created the world went to a lot of trouble. It would be downright rude not to go out and see as much of it as possible."

Edward Readicker-Henderson

November 18

"Every hundred feet the world changes."

Roberto Bolaño, 2666

November 19

"It is always sad to leave a place to which one knows one will never return. Such are the melancolies du voyage: perhaps they are one of the most rewarding things about traveling."

Gustave Flaubert, *Flaubert in Egypt: A Sensibility on Tour*

November 20

According to a Gallup study, people who "always make time for regular trips" had a 68.4 score on the Gallup-Heathway's Well-Being Index, in comparison to a 51.4 Well-Being score for less frequent travelers.

Healthy Set Go

November 21

"Looking at these photographs, I know that I will never understand the world I live in or fully know the places I've been. I've learned for sure only what I don't know—and how much I have to learn."

Anthony Bourdain, *No Reservations*

November 22

"An airport is a potent place, a point of reunions and departures. For the traveler, it's a crossroads at the moment of decision, a flashpoint that separates intention from retreat."

Ginger Bensman, *To Swim Beneath the Earth*

November 23

"If you are choosing between buying your child a tablet or taking them on a family holiday, consider the profound effects on bonding and brain development; there is no competition."

Dr Margot Sunderland, Director of Education and Training at The Centre for Child Mental Health

November 24

"We keep moving forward, opening new doors, and doing new things, because we're curious and curiosity keeps leading us down new paths."

Walt Disney

November 25

"In our perpetual rush to be productive, we often undermine our very ability to consistently perform at peak levels. Getting more done in less time allows us to get ahead and be more productive, but it takes consistent focus to be truly productive. Professional services firm Ernst & Young conducted an internal study of its employees and found that for each additional 10 hours of vacation time employees took, their year-end performance ratings improved 8 percent. What's more, frequent vacationers were significantly less likely to leave the firm."

Lolly Daskal, President and CEO, *Lead From Within*

November 26

"Though we travel the world over to find the beautiful, we must carry it with us or we find it not."

Ralph Waldo Emerson

November 27

"I get butterflies every time I wander beautiful places I've never been."

Katrice Cabral

November 28

"Maybe true travel is not the transportation of the body, but a change of perception, renewing the mind."

Ben Okri, *The Age of Magic*

November 29

"Get your motor runnin',
Head out on the highway,
Lookin' for adventure,
And whatever comes our way."

Steppenwolf, *Born to be Wild*

November 30

"For of this world one never sees enough, and to dine in harmony with nature is one of the gentlest and loveliest things we can do."

James A. Michener, *Iberia*

December

December 1

"Travel is an urge best cultivated from within."

Rough Guides

December 2

"We travel, some of us forever, to seek other states, other lives, other souls."

Anais Nin

December 3

"An ardent desire to go took possession of me once more. Not because I wanted to leave... but because I have always been consumed with one desire; to touch and see as much as possible of the earth and the sea before I die."

Nikos Kazantzakis, *Zorba the Greek*

December 4

"Wherever you go, go with all your heart."

Confucious

December 5

"Travel moulds a man, people mould his wisdom, and experiences mould his life."

Sujit Lalwani, *Life Simplified!*

December 6

"Family holidays are valued by children, both in the moment and for long afterward in their memory."

Oliver James

December 7

"Life offers you a thousand chances...all you have to do is take one."

Frances Mayes, *Under the Tuscan Sun*

December 8

"If we were meant to stay in one place, we would have roots instead of feet."

Rachel Wolchin

December 9

"When you're traveling, you are what you are, right there and then. People don't have your past to hold against you. No yesterdays on the road."

William Least Heat-Moon

December 10

"Come fly with me, let's fly, let's fly away."

Frank Sinatra, *Come Fly With Me*

December 11

"Travel and change of place impart new vigor to the mind."

Seneca

December 12

"Without travels, our existence, our memories, our literature, our dreams, our everything would be very poor, very boring, very limited!"

Mehmet Murat Ildan

December 13

"In his hand are the depths of the earth
The heights of the mountains are his also.
The sea is his, for he made it,
and his hands formed the dry land."

Psalm 95: 4-5

December 14

"Of journeying the benefits are many: the freshness it bringeth to the heart, the seeing and hearing of marvelous things, the delight of beholding new cities, the meeting of unknown friends, and the learning of high manners."

Sadi Gulistan

December 15

"If real, regular, normal, boring life, (when you're at home every day, seeing the same people, doing the same things) is like sitting at home on the floor surrounded by toys... traveling feels to me like going to Toys R Us with your toy box and getting to trade stuff in and buy new things and explore whole new ideas."

Alex Day

December 16

"A lot of us first aspired to far-ranging travel and exotic adventure early in our teens; these ambitions are, in fact, adolescent in nature, which I find an inspiring idea...Thus, when we allow ourselves to imagine as we once did, we know, with a sudden jarring clarity, that if we don't go right now, we're never going to do it. And we'll be haunted by our unrealized dreams and know that we have sinned against ourselves gravely."

Tim Cahill

December 17

"As adults, we countdown to our summer holidays to recharge our batteries. But they can also be a profoundly beneficial time for children. Parents are focused not on work, but on play, thereby giving their children the prized gift of time. Dad or Mum, building sandcastles, playing badminton on the beach, jumping over waves. It seems like fun, but it's also 'attachment play,' and it's vital for bonding. Attachment play also enhances self-esteem, sending a child the psychological message: 'You have my full attention. I delight in you. I delight in being with you.'"

Dr Margot Sunderland, Director of Education and Training at The Centre for Child Mental Health

December 18

"Sun and wind and beat of sea,
Great lands stretching endlessly...
Where be bonds to bind the free?
All the world was made for me!"

Adelaide Crapsey

December 19

"The woods are lovely, dark and deep,
But I have promises to keep,
And miles to go before I sleep,
And miles to go before I sleep."

Robert Frost, *Stopping By Woods On A Snowy Evening*

December 20

"The wish to travel seems to me characteristically human:
the desire to move, to satisfy your curiosity or ease your
fears, to change the circumstances of your life, to be a
stranger, to make a friend, to experience an exotic
landscape, to risk the unknown."

Paul Theroux, *The Tao of Travel*

December 21

"Life is a magical journey, so travel endlessly to unfold its profound and heart touching beauty."

Debasish Mridha

December 22

"A mind that is stretched by a new experience can never go back to its old dimensions."

Oliver Wendell Holmes, Jr.

December 23

"Sail away from the safe harbor. Catch the trade winds in your sails. Explore. Dream. Discover."

H. Jackson Browne Jr., *P.S. I Love You*

December 24

"People travel because it teaches them things they could learn no other way."

Lance Morrow

December 25

"And she brought forth her firstborn son, and wrapped him in swaddling clothes, and laid him in a manger; because there was no room for them in the inn."

Luke 2:7

December 26

"To travel is to take a journey into yourself."

Danny Kaye

December 27

"I travel to be replenished with beauty, for travel makes the beauty of this world seem like a Christmas that never ends."

Carew Papritz, *The Legacy Letters*

December 28

"The world is full of wonderful things you haven't seen yet. Don't ever give up on the chance of seeing them."

J.K. Rowling

December 29

Research shows the biggest boost in happiness comes from planning the vacation. A person can feel the effects up to eight weeks before the trip.

Healthy Set Go

December 30

"There is a whole world out there, waiting for you. A world filled with opportunities wherever and whenever you want to grasp them. And whether you do or you don't.... well that is totally up to you."

Jellis Vaes

December 31

"It is good to have an end to journey toward; but it is the journey that matters, in the end."

Ernest Hemingway

About the Author

A my Hinote is the foun-der and editor in chief of VRM Intel Magazine, which provides news, infor-mation, and resources for the vacation rental industry. With a background in finance and marketing and over thirteen years in the vaca-tion rental industry, Hinote has worked with property  management companies, suppliers, and intermediaries and provides insider information about the growing vacation rental industry.

As a fellow traveler, Hinote has recently completed her second yearlong road trip through Europe, Canada and the United States. Throughout her travels, her appreciation of the many men and women who work in the travel industry is the source of her inspiration for the magazine, the VRM Intel news site, the regional events she hosts, the research that she provides to the travel industry, and this compilation from authors, travelers, poets, songwriters, doctors, academics, and philosophers. Hinote resides in Perdido Key, Florida.